Female and Armed

Female and Armed

A Woman's Guide to Advanced Situational
Awareness, Concealed Carry, and Defensive
Shooting Techniques

Lynne Finch

Foreword by Julianna Crowder

Photos by Christine Kundrat, Don McNeil, and Lynne Finch

Skyhorse Publishing

Skyhorse Publishing books may be purchased in bulk at special discounts for sales promotion, corporate gifts, fund-raising, or educational purposes. Special editions can also be created to specifications. For details, contact the Special Sales Department, Skyhorse Publishing, 307 West 36th Street, 11th Floor, New York, NY 10018 or info@skyhorsepublishing.com.

Skyhorse® and Skyhorse Publishing® are registered trademarks of Skyhorse Publishing, Inc.®, a Delaware corporation.

Visit our website at www.skyhorsepublishing.com.

10 9 8 7 6 5 4 3 2 1

Library of Congress Cataloging-in-Publication Data is available on file.

Cover design by Qualcom Designs
Cover photo credit Thinkstock

Print ISBN: 978-1-63220-525-4
Ebook ISBN: 978-1-63220-911-5

Printed in China

For my students, who inspired me to teach and
encouraged me to never stop learning.

Contents

Table of Figures

Foreword

Women and guns has always been a hot topic in American culture, but women were often typecast as either Annie Oakley or a damsel in distress. Gila Hayes and Paxton Quigley began changing the paradigm in the 90s when they led the charge promoting self-defense tools, accessories, and education. In 2011, a new women's movement started within the firearms industry when social organizations and educational opportunities became tailored for women. Although training techniques did not change much, they began to be presented in a language women related to and understood. Four years later, we are finally seeing products designed for women—not just painted pink, but created with form and function in mind. And, most importantly, we are gaining acceptance among our male counterparts so we don't have to play the Annie or the damsel role, but just ourselves.

According to National Sporting Goods Association's Annual Sports Participation reports, total shooting (hunting and target shooting) participation grew 8.8 percent from 28.4 million in 2006 to 31.0 million in 2013. Participation among men only increased 1.1 percent, while female participation leaped 42 percent! So what exactly happened to awaken so many women? There are several plausible answers and that is the beauty of this "Golden Age for Female Gun Owners" as Kathy Jackson of *The Cornered Cat* has named it. Women have joined for self-defense, recreation, and/or athletic sport, and have made a tremendous impact on the shooting industry.

In 2014 the National Shooting Sports Foundation (NSSF) commissioned a comprehensive study to understand female gun owners' behaviors and attitudes that influences their participation in shooting activities. The study also looked at social and environmental factors that create both opportunities and barriers to women shooting. The resulting NSSF report "Women Gun Owners: Purchasing, Perceptions, and Participation" by Laura Kippen, president of the research firm InfoManiacs, stated: "This research yielded a variety of key takeaways that, when implemented, should keep the trend of female participation in shooting activities moving upward."

The NSSF study analyzed responses from 1,000 women on a variety of topics from where women purchase guns, where they get training, and purchasing plans and preferences. The report concluded that women that had some form of firearms training were both spending and participating more than women that did not have training.

An organization that provides training and encourages long-term participation is A Girl & A Gun Women's Shooting League (AG & AG). When I founded the club in early 2011, the intention was to have a place for women to gather for a

"Girl's Night Out" at the range for fellowship, fun, and of course, development of important life skills in regards to firearms. The organization grew nationally only a short six months after its inception to eighty chapters across the country at the close of 2014.

I witnessed the first wave of women introduced to firearms settling in and figuring out how they fit into a historically male-dominated activity, while the second, third, and fourth waves jumped into welcoming arms of ranges and retailers. The firearms industry continued to reach out to women shooters; however, they were having their own awakening that women needed gender-specific products and that they had significant purchasing power in the market. It has been an exciting time to work together with other leading women to change views in the industry.

Lynne Finch is not only a leader in this latest women's movement, but she is a trailblazer as well. Lynne burst onto the national scene in June 2012 with Take Your Daughter to the Range Day (known today as Daughters at the Range). When the industry was beginning to focus on women, she turned the spotlight towards the next generation of firearm owners—our daughters! Her contributions to the women's movement also include two previous books, *Taking Your First Shot* and *The Home Security Handbook*, which guide women through the maze of ownership, education, and personal responsibility. Her third installment, *Female and Armed* takes you to the next level by exploring the question, "What's next to learn?" Oh, there is so much to learn!

As you read along, you will find that Lynne's delivery is a comfortable, approachable conversation with a friend about a very serious topic. She revisits fundamentals and answers many questions that women shooters may encounter in their training: *What are the variations of ammunition? Why do I need that gun or this accessory? What do I do if I have to go hand-to-hand with an attacker?* This guide helps you develop your personal training plan so that you do not respond to a threat as a damsel in distress. Instead, Lynne gives you knowledge, correct terminology, and the confidence of Annie Oakley to walk into a class full of our male counterparts and excel!

Julianna Crowder
Founder & President
A Girl and A Gun Women's Shooting League, LLC
www.AGirlandAGun.org

Introduction

In my first book, *Taking Your First Shot*, I wrote about how much fun shooting is and how to get started. I also added some basic self-defense moves that are easy and that you don't have to have ninja-level skills to accomplish. This book came about because so many women wrote to ask for something with more advanced techniques. So after lots of research and practice (I didn't want to suggest anything I was too afraid to try, couldn't do, or that didn't work for me . . . I'm not in great shape, have my share of achy places, and have a healthy fear of breaking something that comes with being over forty and finding out I don't bounce like I did when I was twenty), here we are . . . *Female and Armed*—packed full of advanced defensive techniques for women—some are with a gun, some without. But I want to emphasize here, and you will see this again:

YOUR BEST DEFENSE IS TO NOT NEED A DEFENSE!

What does that mean? You are aware, you are alert, and you make every effort to avoid the situation that requires an armed or physical response. Anytime you find yourself in one of those situations, you are at serious risk of injury or even death. That is the harsh reality. Be prepared, learn the skills, but use your situational awareness and your intuition to the maximum extent possible. Practicing can be a lot of fun, but the reality of a confrontation can be harsh. If you find yourself in a bad situation that requires a response, do just enough to get away. This isn't about being tough, strong, or even afraid. Staying in a fight after you have a chance to get away changes everything. The longer you are in a confrontation, the greater the risk of you being injured or killed. If you had a chance to escape and didn't, that may also taint your position under the law. Don't put yourself in more danger—do what you have to do to escape and then call the police. Always call the police as soon as you have reached safety. Better they hear your side first and start looking for your attacker than to hear from someone else about the "crazy lady" screaming in the parking lot. At that point, they are looking for you and not the criminals, giving them time to go assault someone else.

I've often told the story of going to the grocery store with my husband and asking him to wait for a minute before we left so I could get my gun. His response was, "We are going to the grocery store." The "duh" was implied. I pointed out that if we were going somewhere I thought I would need the gun, why would we go there? Think about that—why go somewhere where you are likely to have a dangerous encounter? As for the places that seem safe, don't be complacent, stay alert, and be prepared. Bad things can happen anywhere.

Even though the title reads for women, the techniques are mostly gender neutral. The biggest difference is that this book is written by a woman with a female audience in mind. So it is okay to share with your male friends—just warn them some of the humor may need to be explained. No man bashing intended, but sometimes they just don't understand.

You will see and read about some techniques here that are potentially dangerous. These will be called out as last resort options. When you believe you are at risk of serious injury or death, some of these might be what you need to save your life, but there is a risk and a possibility that you could get hurt. The people in the photos are all professional instructors with lots of practice and training behind them. Even so, not everyone was willing to try everything, and that is ok. Work to your level of comfort, and as you build your skills you can do more. These techniques will come with a warning, Do Not Try This at Home! So hold on—I tell you how to do something and then tell you not to try it—how are you supposed to learn it? I will address the use of training aids and training partners. Blue guns, training knives, Muy Thai pads . . . all of these will help you to learn and practice these techniques in relative safety.

I want to say a special thank you to Skyhorse Publishing for believing in me and supporting me. Kristin, who is the best editor ever, thank you for your patience and encouragement. To my training team—Amy, Judit, Judy, Kathleen, Ed, Noah, and John—I could never have gotten through this without you. Your willingness to jump in and try things, suggestions, support, and most of all your humor made this work possible.

Christine and Don, two awesome photographers who gave freely of their time and skills, thank you! Christine is responsible for some of the amazing photos that she captured with a high-speed camera, such as the muzzle flash from my GLOCK or the brass tumbling through the air.

Thank you John, of FPF Training, for the use of your range to try some things that we couldn't have done anywhere else. It was a beautiful day, spectacular range, and the best part was, after the photos, we got to play! You can see a video of Kathleen making a water jug dance on my YouTube channel, Female and Armed. There is no better way to experience the sheer joy of shooting than a perfect day on a beautiful range with skilled friends and lots of guns and ammo to share. I shot Noah's .308 rifle, put two rounds through one hole, and decided to quit while I was ahead. Sometimes you just need to smile and take the win.

Thank you to friends and family who listened to ideas, put up with my not going out because "I have to work on the book," and who gave me encouragement and kept me going. The women who emailed me, came up to talk to me at events, or messaged me on Facebook to ask for this . . . without you this book wouldn't exist. This is my third book in as many years, so they've been really patient. I hope you find useful, thought provoking, and fun information between these covers. I love it when readers write to me; you can find my contact information in the back. Send me your stories, thoughts, and questions.

Be safe, be aware, and train like your life may depend on it.

Lynne

1. What to Expect

S ome say, "Your best defense is a good offense." I can support that if by offense you mean there isn't a need to defend yourself. I am assuming if you are reading this book that you already have some experience with a firearm. If not, you may want to go back and start with *Taking*

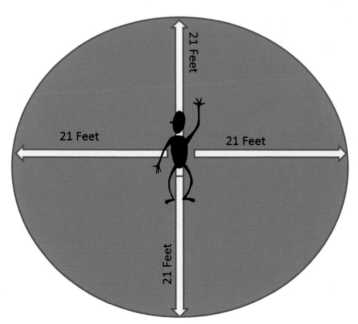

Figure 1 - Safety Circle

Your First Shot. Female and Armed is written for those who have some experience with firearms and understand the basic concepts of situational awareness. However, let's talk about situational awareness, just so we are together on this. You see, not just with your eyes but with all of your senses, what is happening around you. I defined the safety circle based on the well-known Tueller Drill; how fast can someone close a distance of twenty-one feet? Pretty fast—two to three seconds! That doesn't give you much time to respond, so it is really your minimum for awareness. You need to be aware of what is around you and what is happening. Is someone looking at you? Does something feel wrong? Trust your instincts and get out! Don't hesitate because you might be wrong.

Better to be Safe and Wrong than to be Right and in Danger

Lieutenant Colonel Jeff Cooper was a combat veteran Marine and founder of the American Pistol Institute. One of his many significant contributions is the Cooper Color Code.

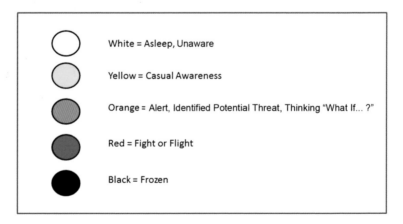

White = Asleep, Unaware

Yellow = Casual Awareness

Orange = Alert, Identified Potential Threat, Thinking "What If... ?"

Red = Fight or Flight

Black = Frozen

Figure 2 - Situational Awareness Color Code Chart

Condition White is oblivious, asleep, or completely unaware. Think of the person walking down the street, head down, and texting away who steps off the curb and into traffic. They may be on the phone, listening to music, or reading a book. What they share is a lack of situational awareness, and this makes them easy targets.

Condition Yellow is aware, head up, confident, and casually scanning your surroundings. You are not on high alert, but you are aware of potential threats in your immediate area. It does not matter if you are ten or eighty years of age, projecting confidence in your walk and attitude can dramatically reduce your risk of an attack or, at the very least, give you some warning that it is coming so you can prepare.

Condition Orange is when something catches your eye that is not quite right. You may feel the hair on the back of your neck go up or have an unsettled feeling in your stomach. Pay attention, something is off! It may be someone coming toward you. Criminal flash mobs are a current danger where a group of seemingly random people suddenly swarms together as a mob to wreak havoc. If you see people milling about and then they appear to catch each other's eyes, all check their phones at the same time, or start to move together . . . get out fast! You may see someone paying a little too much attention to you and then glancing toward another person—they could be a team targeting you. You may sense someone is following you while you are driving. You are in Condition Orange; you have noticed a potential threat. Now start thinking of "what if . . ." scenarios. What will I do if he suddenly starts toward me? What will I do if that random group starts to move together? What will I do when I notice that car behind me has been there for a while? Even if nothing happens, practicing the "what if . . ." helps you to begin to think about your response and keeping yourself safe. The more you practice "what if . . ." the easier and faster the response becomes. Sound hard? You probably do this every day while driving. Ever just have a feeling the car in the next lane was about to do something stupid, such as change lanes and try to occupy the same space as you? No signal, no over the shoulder glance, but you could tell and started making decisions about your reaction—maybe slowing down to make a space or speeding up to get in front of them. That is situational awareness, and it is also shifting from yellow to orange. You know something isn't right, and you start thinking of what you can do if they make a move.

Condition **Red** is the fight-or-flight stage. The threat is there, you must take action . . . fast. You can move from yellow to orange to red very quickly, but as you become used to being aware, you will recognize situations that have the potential to turn bad and will give yourself more time to prepare. Later we will discuss various options for what I prefer to think of as the fight-and-flight response, but the key is recognizing the threat before it is too close, planning your response, and then taking action, thereby avoiding Condition Black.

Condition **Black** is when you freeze. Time seems to stop, you cannot move, cannot think, and cannot respond. This happens to everyone at some point, but you must recognize it so you can shake it off and get back to response mode. Condition Black can be extremely dangerous and very frightening. Just remember, it may feel like minutes but actually last only seconds, and you need to push through so you can protect yourself. Condition Black was not part of the original Cooper Color Code but was added later to help people identify that moment of panic when they freeze and prepare for it.

Being aware and using your brain are the first steps to keeping yourself safe. Innocent victims are not dumb, but they may be naïve. They did not see the attack coming. They were not situationally aware. Keep your head up, your eyes open, and be alert. You will look more confident, more in control, and taller! You will also project to the bad guy that you are not an easy target. For many criminals, this is how they make a living. They don't want to be injured and unable to work, they want the easiest victim possible. Don't give it to them!

When the worst happens, trust your instincts. Yell, fight, draw your firearm . . . use what you have to, but ONLY what you have to, to give yourself a chance to escape. Remember that proportional response is a smart thing—meeting force with like force. You do not want the legal system to see you as the aggressor. Like force can vary with the circumstances, as a petite woman may be justified in using harsher measures against a six-foot, two-hundred-pound attacker but not against a female aggressor of similar stature.

A common phenomenon is second-guessing yourself after a situation. This is normal, but if you aren't expecting it, it can be quite devastating. Many years ago I was in the US Air Force and stationed in Korea. I had the attitude that went with being in my twenties: I was indestructible, in good shape, nothing bad would happen to me. I used to hike in the hills beyond the base where I was stationed and often went several hours without seeing another person.

One day I came across a Korean man. The Korean people are generally polite and generous, so I was not concerned. He attempted to talk to me, although his English was quite limited, and my Korean was mostly limited to greetings and thank you. Between words and gestures, I realized he was offering me money for sex. About seven dollars, actually. It was probably all he had, or so I have convinced myself. At first I thought it was funny, then I was a little offended. (I'm still not sure which bothered me more, the supposition that I could be bought or the amount, as the going rate for a professional was twenty dollars at the time.) I declined and kept walking . . . he grabbed my arm and turned me back toward him. Then he grabbed me between my legs. I had taken lots of self-defense classes and attended many lectures and seminars. In that moment I didn't think of anything except getting him off me and running. I hit him hard, both hands square in the chest, knocking him off his feet, and I took off. That night, I started thinking of the training and all the things I could have done. I began to question myself—why didn't I do more, why didn't I use this or that technique? I endured the nightmares and emotional torment for a couple days before I talked to a counselor. She said just the right thing, "You did just enough to get away safely." I didn't make it worse, I didn't underreact, I did just enough. It was like the clouds parted and it was sunny again. I was safe, I didn't hurt anyone, I defended myself . . . I really did use a technique I had learned.

Why am I sharing this story? I told this story in a basic self-defense class, and when I was done I realized a student had tears in her eyes. At the break I asked if she was OK. She told me that something similar had happened to her, and she thought she was the only one to go through the process of reliving the attack and second guessing every move. The tears were an emotional reaction to realizing that it was a normal response.

I was the lucky one. I found a caring, smart counselor who said exactly what I needed to hear. I hope you never have to experience this kind of trauma, but if you do . . . do the minimum you have to in order to get away. Don't make the situation worse, and don't put yourself in physical or legal jeopardy. Make a moment to escape and get out of there. Then remember you got away, you didn't make it worse, and you didn't do anything wrong. You did just enough, and that is the best response.

2. Should You Carry a Firearm?

I f you are fortunate enough to live in a state that permits concealed carry, you still have a big decision to make. I encourage all of my students to apply for their permits even if they never intend to carry just to make it easier to transport firearms to and from the range. But you need to ask yourself, should you carry a gun for self-defense? Only you can know the answer to that, but it is an answer you need to know before you ever walk out the door wearing a gun.

Are you prepared to use lethal force if needed to defend yourself or your family? Have you considered the risks: legal, physical, and yes, even moral? Are you prepared to make that tough decision to pull the trigger without hesitation if you believe you are facing an imminent threat of severe bodily harm or death? A gun is not a good luck charm, and it doesn't somehow inoculate us against bad things that happen to good people. If you have any doubt about your ability to shoot, don't carry a gun until you are certain. Understand that the mere sight of a gun probably will not be enough to deter an attack. It might, but . . . what if it doesn't and you have not made the decision? The time to make the decision is not when you are frightened; it is when you are calm. You need to make the decision you can live with before you need it. You need to be prepared for the response from family, friends, and law enforcement. Have a gun-friendly attorney selected in advance just in case. Understand that adrenaline tends to make us run off at the mouth. Be prepared to cooperate with the police but to say you were in fear for your life, and little else, until you have calmed down. In the adrenaline overload, you may not even remember what you are saying, but the police are capturing every word. Give yourself time to calm down before giving a detailed account of what happened—it needs to be accurate.

Some women tell me they wouldn't hesitate to use a gun to defend their child. However, they do hesitate when asked about defending themselves. It may be cliché, but defending yourself is defending your family. It you aren't there for them . . . well, I don't want to consider it.

Think about it, and spend the time to soul search for the answer. Once you know, you will know if that is the right answer for you. For me, it was a quick decision. But I had been threatened, and I was prepared for a him-or-me scenario. I may go down, but it won't be easy. If you haven't faced that, it might be a harder decision.

I encourage you to remember that you are important to someone and someone loves you and wants you here. You should love you as well. I am important enough to defend for me, for my friends, and for my family.

There are fundamentals that you need to understand if you are going to carry a gun. These need to be well under-stood so you don't have to think about them in the moment.

- Know your target and what is beyond it. Bullets, even hollow points, can overpenetrate and keep going. There is no guarantee that your round will stay in your target.
- Understand what is near your target. Look at the statistics, as even trained professionals miss under stressful conditions.
- Understand that pulling the trigger changes two lives forever.
- Understand that you may face legal action and can be expected to be arrested while things are sorted out.

Do these things stop me from carrying a gun? No. But I practice, and I understand the risks and the need to have more than one option for response depending on the situation. My gun is not my first choice, it is last resort. Do I want to shoot another human being? No! Would I if my life were in danger and it was him or me? Yes. That was not an easy decision, and not everyone can make it. Just because it was a decision I made quickly did not mean it was easy. You need to find the answer that is in your heart, and only then will you know if you can carry a gun. Not carrying doesn't mean you can't still shoot. Many people enjoy the recreational aspects of the shooting sports but never consider carrying a gun.

3. Myths

Carrying a gun means I will never need to use it.

FALSE! Carrying a gun means you can use it if you have to, but it is not a charm or rabbit's foot. It doesn't stop bad things from happening to good people.

I'm older, out of shape. . . . I can't really defend myself in an up close and personal attack.

FALSE! Look at the photos in this book. At the time these photos were taken, I was fifty-five with two artificial knees and overweight. Many of the ladies who helped have something that slows them down (except Judit, she is in great shape, and Amy is really strong). What do we have in common? Training! We know how to work around our limitations. You don't have to be young and buff to take care of yourself. With my knees, I know an ankle holster is not a good option for me; I don't get up and down easily. Judy has found ways to compensate for being more petite, OK . . . short. The bottom line is that we all were able to use these techniques to defend against an attack and come out intact, we just had to adapt them slightly to fit our individual needs and limitations.

If I show the gun to the bad guy, I can scare him into leaving me alone.

FALSE! Don't bet your life on it. He may see the gun, see your hesitation, and think "Ooh, I can get a shiny new gun for me." If you carry a gun, you MUST be prepared to use it. Otherwise, you are potentially supplying your own instrument of destruction. Also, showing the gun without the intent to use it may be considered brandishing by the law.

The bottom line here? Young, old, heavy, skinny, fit, out of shape, physically challenged . . . there are things we can all do to save ourselves. Practice and get coaching or more formal training if you want it. There are many ways to be effective in your response, but you have to be committed to your own safety.

4. Training Aids

Nothing beats practice for developing a skill. But practice with a weapon isn't always feasible. This is where training aids are invaluable. A blue gun, a solid piece of plastic that can be purchased in replicas of most popular models of firearm, is incredibly effective for training. You can draw from a holster, you can wrestle on the ground, and you can grapple for it to practice retention techniques. (Note: ALWAYS keep your finger off the trigger when practicing because if it is inside the trigger guard and the gun is twisted out of your hand, your finger can easily be broken.) You can even, with permission, point it toward another person, which you should **never** do with a real gun unless you intend to shoot them. I don't care how many times you think you checked that it wasn't loaded . . . *do not do it!* What are the first words most often said after a negligent discharge? "I didn't think the gun was loaded!"

During the photo session for this book, a very experienced instructor was on the ground with a blue gun and rolling over to point it at her attacker. She didn't realize that she was sweeping her own leg, which meant she could potentially

Figure 3 - GLOCK 19 Next to Blue Gun

have shot herself in the thigh had it been a real life situation. Those of us watching spotted it and worked with her until she could roll and draw without sweeping herself. It helps to train with a friend or two, and we all learned from that. But had it not been a training gun, the results could have been disastrous!

I took handgun retention training from an instructor I have a lot of respect for, and we used blue guns, but not without a safety briefing and informed consent. She would no more have considered teaching with real firearms than we would have considered using them for training. If you ever find yourself in a class where the instructor tells you to point a firearm at another person . . . leave immediately! There are two exceptions: one is a class that uses air guns and the other is simunitions training. These are highly specialized and

Figure 4 - Know Where Your Gun is Pointed

involve special firearms and protective equipment to train in force on force. This is advanced training, and you should research the instructors offering it before taking any class like this to ensure they have good safety records and are certified to teach these types of classes.

Sight Indicating Resetting Trigger, or SIRT, guns make great training aids because you can see where your shot hit. They project a laser, which is not eye-safe so be careful of people and pets, that you can see on a target or wall. This is especially helpful for the nonideal shooting positions. If you are at full extension, you will not see the dot, as it shines from just below the barrel, so a spotter is helpful. But for those unusual positions, such as from the ground or with your arm bent and tucked into your side, it is ideal. As an extra bonus, if you have cats, they love chasing the laser dot! All I have to say to my girls is "Dot!" and they come running ready to play.

Figure 5 - SIRT

Another great aid is a training knife. Knives are scary, and many people are more afraid of them than they are of guns. In my disarming training, I can see why. It is nearly impossible to disarm someone who has a knife without getting cut. A training knife has a dulled edge so that it can't cut anything! They tend to have brightly colored handles, which make them easily distinguished from real knives. Most also have holes in the blade so that it cannot be sharpened. I've also created a training knife by dulling down the blade on a real knife but only because I couldn't find a replica in that type of knife. If you are using a training knife, double check the edge each and every time, and *do not* carry a real knife at the same time. In the stress of the moment you could reach for the wrong knife with potentially disastrous results. Don't think you would never do that, as professionals have made that mistake even with years of training.

A Muy Thai pad is a great aid for practicing strikes. Your partner holds the pad, and you can wail away on it without causing injury. Just don't miss! I accidently caught my defense instructor in the ribs with an elbow. I felt really bad about it. After he caught his breath, he told me it was all his fault—his attention slipped for a moment—but that it confirmed

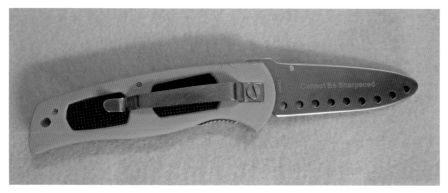

Figure 6 - Training Knife 1

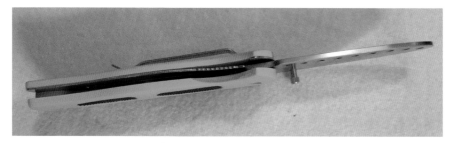

Figure 7 - Training Knife 2

for him I wasn't pulling my punches . . . Actually I was, but I didn't have the heart to tell him at that point. If you don't have a training partner handy, I find a hanging heavy bag is also very effective and a great way to get rid of stress. (Mine is pink!)

Training aids allow you to practice in safety. If you really want to have fun, get some oversized white T-shirts and some washable markers. Think you can handle yourself against someone, even someone inexperienced, with a knife? You and your training partner can spar with the markers. They wash out and off the skin, so you can do it over and over. You will be amazed at how many "cuts" you have. Use two colors so

Figure 8 - Muy Thai Pad

you can see how many times you cut yourself! I was shocked the first time I tried this—I had almost as many cuts from me as from my partner! This might make you think twice about your abilities to avoid the knife. It was an eye-opening experience but also a lot of fun. If your opponent has some skills or training, most likely the knife will always be in motion, slashing, thrusting, and moving so fast it is hard to track. This is extremely difficult to defend against, and you will get cut. It's better to understand what you might be facing than

Figure 9 - My Pink Heavy Bag

to be surprised. Hollywood has not done us a lot of favors, and the bad guy doesn't always hold the knife still, looking menacing, and then thrust.

5. Equipment

Defensive shooting needs specialized equipment. Like any sport—not that defensive shooting is a sport, but shooting is—there are a wide range of options but following are some minimums.

You need a good holster. What makes a good holster? First, it provides good retention for your gun. It is accessible, you'll use it, and it doesn't pinch or poke you in places that cause pain or blisters. How do you know what is best for you? Trial and error seems to be the most common approach. I prefer a holster without additional retention devices, just like I prefer my handguns without manual safeties, which are something else to remember and cope with in an emergency.

While there are a lot of options out there, my personal favorites come from Looper Law Enforcement, home of the Flashbang holster line, and from Femme Fatale Holsters. My number one favorite is the Ava from Flashbang, which is a hybrid in the waist holster that fits me perfectly. The leather isn't cut as high on the backside as most holsters of that style, so it doesn't dig in the ribs, and it has a lovely suede backing that is pretty and comfortable. Many people say a holster is never comfortable, but I disagree. This is my favorite for my primary carry gun, which is a GLOCK 19. It is surprisingly comfortable, gives good retention, and is pretty easy to conceal. If for some reason I can't carry in the waistband, I may go to a smaller firearm and switch to a Flashbang, which tucks under the bra, or to a thigh band from Femme Fatale. They are sturdy with a pocket for the gun, a strong stretchy fabric, and sexy lace overlay. It takes a little getting used to, but they conceal beautifully! I wear it on my opposite leg with the gun on the inner thigh so I can draw easily with my strong hand. Femme Fatale Holsters also makes a corset style that doubles as a support garment so you can access your gun from above and some pretty ankle holsters. Just remember, if you are going to use an ankle holster, you need the flexibility to drop quickly to one knee and deploy your firearm. It helps if you are also able to get back up fast to give yourself a better chance to move. This is why I don't use ankle holsters—I can't move that way. In the time it would take me to get up from a kneeling position, an attacker could close the distance, knock me over, and still have time to call his BFF and make dinner plans. Know your limitations, and be honest with yourself.

Those are my top picks, but you might like something different. Holsters are like shoes, they need to feel right to you. You do want to be consistent in your carry as much as possible, but I recognize that isn't always feasible.

The second thing you absolutely need is a gun belt. If you are carrying on the waist, you need a belt designed to

Figure 10 - Flashbang's The AVA

Figure 11 - The Flashbang Holster

Figure 12 - Femme Fatale's Thigh Band

support the holster and the gun. These things are heavy, and the pretty little belts we find in the women's department won't safely support that weight. My personal favorites, and again these are just options, are also from Flashbang. They are heavy duty leather with pretty suede backs. I suggest getting a belt that is a little larger than you think you need and having an extra hole or two punched, which any shoe repair shop can do for you. The belts are expensive, and if you get it a little big, you can wear it with more things, such as on the waist or further down the hip with lower rise pants.

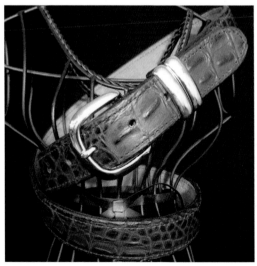

Figure 13 - Flashbang's Hello Sailor Belt

Figure 14 - Flashbang's MissBehavin Belt

If you carry in a purse, which is not my preferred method because you really have to keep close track of it, make sure you have a carry purse that has a holster built in. There are some really pretty options now. Many have reinforced shoulder straps that can be lengthened for cross-body carry. Most have a quick access point to get to the gun, and it is possible with some of them to shoot without removing the gun. Of course it is harder and will ruin the purse, but if you are in a hurry . . . well, it is an option. Do not drop a gun into a regular purse to carry it. You never know which direction it is pointed, where it is—except that it is likely on the bottom because it is heavier than anything else—and what is going to be sticking out of it if you do have to draw it. Anyone need

Figure 15 - Gun Purse

a pen? Pens can slip into the barrel or, worse, into the trigger guard easily, as can keys, lipsticks, and anything small. Plus, if you are the victim of a purse snatching, you've not only lost your purse but also your gun!

Other key equipment? Options! Your gun is a last resort. Do you have pepper spray? Do you know how to use it? Spray back and forth, aiming for the eyebrows so it will run into the eyes, in 3–5 second bursts. Where is your pepper spray? Hopefully not at the bottom of your purse with your keys, as it should be in your hand or quickly accessible when you are out and about. Have you ever practiced with it? Don't try this on a windy day, but you should know what it feels like to flick the safety and press the button. You should also know the spray will come out in the direction you intend it to. Pepper spray has an expiration date on it, so check yours. If you have had it for several years, it may be a great practice spray but not so good for an aggressor.

Personal alarms are great attention getters. They make a lot of noise and can draw attention to you in a bad situation. Look for one with a pin activation so you can grab the alarm and throw it, while pulling the pin in the process. I have mine on a clasp that I hang on the outside of my purse. That way I can grab the alarm, yank, and toss. Why? It will keep making noise for several minutes, and if I keep it in my hand, the bad guy could potentially get it from me and smash it to silence the noise. If I throw it, it is less likely that he will be able to get to it to silence it. SabreRed makes a sleek little no-nonsense alarm that easily attaches to your bag, keys, belt . . . and it makes a lot of noise. It is about the size of a thumb drive and works great.

Flashlights, the tactical kind such as 5.11 or Fenix, are great. Not only can you use it if the lights go off, you can use it to destroy the night vision of someone coming at you in the dark, which buys time to run away. I once found myself in a parking garage during a power outage. I was the only one who could find my car! But you can blast someone in the face with the light, temporarily blinding them in the dark. Just remember to step off to the side when you do so you are not where they last saw you.

Figure 16 - Tactical Flashlight

Noise, your voice, a whistle, and yelling "Stranger!" can attract unwanted attention to your attacker and hopefully make them change their mind. If someone is approaching, it is ok to put your hand up and say "STOP." Use your drill sergeant or mom voice. (Is there a difference?) Let them know you are not an easy target. A dainty, soft little "Please stop" is more likely to keep them coming than to stop them. When you are in danger, or when you think you might be, is NOT the time to worry about being polite or ladylike.

Are you sensing a theme? Avoidance! Contact is the last thing you want, and the personal and legal complications that come with pulling the trigger are a lot to deal with, even when you are clearly in the right. There is a saying, "When you pull the trigger, two lives are changed forever." Even if the situation doesn't escalate to the gun, you are at risk for injury if there is physical contact. Better off not risking it if you can avoid it at all.

6. Defensive Shooting Stance

If you are primarily a range shooter and have only taken basic classes, odds are good you shoot in the isosceles position, where your feet are parallel and your arms form a triangle. There isn't anything wrong with that, and most of us start that way. But as you move more into the world of defensive shooting, you will want to change your stance so you are ready to move at a moment's notice. Think of how fighters or football players stand; their feet are usually offset and shoulder width apart with one forward of the other. This is so they can react and move quickly. You can't do that when your feet are parallel. Practice the stance and

Figure 17 - Isosceles Shooting Position

moving in all directions. Be aware so you are not crossing your feet like a grapevine dance step, where you cross one foot over or behind the other, which can cause you to trip. Do not move backward without being sure you know what is there. You do not want to trip on a curb and fall because you were backing away and didn't look. You do not need a gun in your hand to practice this—you can do it anywhere. Sometimes I practice on the elevator but only when I'm alone.

Figure 18 - Defensive Stance

Your ideal position may not be possible; you may be shooting across your body, with a bent arm, one handed, with your nondominant hand, or even from the ground. You need to practice these positions as much as you can, even if only with a blue gun to increase your level of confidence in case you need them. Knocking a woman to the ground is a common tactic because the bad guy mistakenly thinks that it will be easier to subdue her. Don't buy into that, you can fight from the ground! **A key point here—*this is why I don't encourage small-of-the-back carry!*** If you get knocked to the ground, there is a high risk you will land on your back and on your gun. That alone could cause serious injury, but it also makes it extremely difficult to get to your gun.

Figure 19 - Fighting from the Ground

Think of all the things we do in our daily lives. Can you access a firearm, aim, and shoot from all of those positions? What about in the car? Is your gun blocked by a seatbelt? Is it stashed in the glove compartment, where you can't get to it quickly? Is it in a holster on the steering column? See the chapter on carjacking for more specific information and suggestions.

What about if you are in bed? Do you have quick access safe storage near the bed, or is the gun in a safe in the basement? What do you do when you hear the crash of breaking glass or your door being kicked in? Can you kneel by the bed and shoot? Crouch on the floor?

What about sitting on the sofa watching TV? Not carrying? With home invasions on the rise, you may want to reconsider

Figure 20 - Gun Vault Quick Access Gun Safe

that. More and more people have incorporated on-body carry into their everyday lives, both at home and away.

Basically, you want to get comfortable drawing and deploying a firearm from any position you might find yourself in. It doesn't have to be graceful, but it does need to be safe. While we are talking about being safe, can you identify your target AND what is beyond it in a flash? You are in the bedroom, and you hear someone coming up the stairs, but the line of fire leads straight through your child's room. Do you take the shot? You are using defensive hollow-point ammunition, right? That should be safe, right? Wrong! I have taped six layers of drywall together to form a block. The bullet made a small neat hold going in and a jagged disintegrating mess coming out from the last layer. Is it possible to fire a round in your home, have it go through the exterior wall and across the street, and enter the next house? YES! You need to know what is beyond your target BEFORE you pull the trigger. That is easy at the range because there is a backstop or a berm. In real life, that backstop could be a school bus or a family. Shooting is a risk, especially defensive shooting, which is why you need to be sure before you pull the trigger. Does this mean I'm going to hesitate? No, this is what makes situational awareness so critical. You need to plan for what you can, such as relatively safe directions in your home, and then be aware of your surroundings when you are out so you can plan a safe direction and spot a confrontation before it happens. Remember, the gun is a tool of *last resort!* Only shoot if you have to. But if you have to, be sure you have trained so you know what to do and how to do it, and practice regularly so you know you can hit your target.

7. Range Drills

Now we get into the fun stuff: shooting! To be safe, you need to practice. Shooting is a perishable skill, and if you don't go to the range and train, you may not be able to hit your target in an emergency. To be clear, don't make every trip to the range about training hard—sometimes you just need to have fun making holes in paper, pinging steel, or making the water jug dance, depending on your range and preferred target. Spice it up. Tape playing cards to your target and see if you can hit the markings. Draw shapes on your target or use stickers. I buy sheets of half-inch round stickers at the office supply store that I can put on plain paper, and that becomes my target. A really good day is when I shoot through the sticker and it falls off, and then I put a few more rounds through the same hole.

If you are somewhere where you can, try shooting nontraditional targets, such as water jugs, watermelons, and Kevlar clipboards. . . . There is a range in Virginia that lets people bring in junk appliances and cars to shoot up. Tired of doing laundry? Take that, washing machine! I have a friend who haunts yard sales to get Barbie and GI Joe dolls to use as targets. I once put a few rounds through an old hard drive. That is one way to get rid of data! Years ago, I took flying lessons. My instructor told me, "Sometimes you need to make holes in the clouds." He was telling me to stop focusing so hard on learning the next step and have fun once in a while. Shooting is fun, or we wouldn't do it, so don't push yourself too hard. As long as you are hitting the target, you are training.

The NRA Winchester Marksmanship program is a great way to train. It is self-paced; it takes you through things you need to know, such as one-hand and weak-hand shooting, as well as helping you to build your confidence and your skill. Plus, if you are as geeky as I am, you can get great patches and pins for each level you complete! To the right is the top of one of my range bags. It gets a bit of attention, as relatively few people get the last rocker. It took time and dedication, but I learned so much that I recommend the program to shooters all the time.

The scan is an important aspect of defensive training. Always remember if you see one assailant, there are probably two. If you see three, there are probably four. To scan, bring your gun back into a High Compressed Ready (HCR) position and,

Figure 21 - Marksmanship Patches

keeping it pointed downrange, quickly—but not blurry fast—look over each shoulder to see what is behind you. Go fast enough that you don't lose track of what is in front of you and slow enough to process the information behind you. What are people wearing? Is someone watching? If you are shooting with a buddy, you can have your partner stand behind you while changing positions so you don't know where they will

Figure 22 - HCR

Figure 23 - Scanning for Threats

Figure 24 - Buddy Shoot 1

Figure 25 - Buddy Shoot 2

be, and they can hold up fingers to indicate the number of shots you should take next. A closed fist can mean slow down and go for the head shot. One, two, or three fingers can mean that many shots to the high-center chest. If you look and see you partner, don't neglect the other direction. Check both sides so you don't get in a habit of just looking one way.

You can also have someone behind you pelting you with cold brass or yelling and stressing you. This helps you learn to center your focus on the task and block out the distraction, which is a potentially valuable skill in an emergency situation.

When we were doing photos for this book, one of the aggressors snuck up and screamed at the women on the line. Their reactions were genuine; they were startled. This happens. Some of us are more easily startled than others, but they were comfortable since we were all friends, and we were not expecting something to go wrong . . . *you never know!*

Figure 26 - Ed Scaring the Gang

Situational awareness of his location and their surroundings could have minimized their reactions.

One of the drills we did that your range may not allow was close contact. With my hand on the shoulder of the target, braced as if I were pushing off an attacker, I drew and fired point blank into the abdomen. There is a small risk if you aren't 100 percent certain where your muzzle is. This is one that might best be practiced with a blue gun. But you should be prepared if the threat is close. Can you hold them back while you get to your gun, fire with your elbow tucked in close to your body, and shoot at point blank range? If your range allows it, you can practice shooting from that position with your arm tight to your body to maximize control. It is a different feeling than the traditional fully extended position. It was also a lot of fun—after the first one, I hustled to the next target to do it again. There was something about the paper exploding out that back that made it more fun. In training, many of the instructors found they took their push-off hand away before firing. When I asked why, the answer was generally that is was too close to where they were shooting. In reality, it was probably more than twelve inches, and when you are three inches from your target, that is a lot of distance. Be comfortable knowing the direction of your muzzle based on the feel of the gun in your hand so you can shoot with confidence without being at full extension or having the ability to see the firearm. You need to feel how and where you are aiming. Practice this with a blue gun if that's more comfortable. Draw and get the gun into position then look in a mirror. Is it where you thought it was pointed? Practice until you know, just by the feel of your wrist and hand, exactly where your gun is pointed. You aren't going to be shooting distances like this—only inches—so you do have some margin for error, but you need to know where the gun is pointed relative to your body and to the attacker. One thing to consider is that this does put you in a vulnerable position if your attacker has any skills. Some self-defense schools will teach pushing off and backing away to put some distance between you and your attacker before you draw to make it more difficult for the bad guy to get your gun. This is a valid point, but it is also situational. You need to understand your level of skill and be able to make that decision fast. If you can hit him

Figure 27 - Close Quarters Drill

and get some distance, great, if not . . . you may need to be prepared to shoot from inches.

If your range allows, you need to get used to drawing from the holster and shooting. You come straight up until the gun clears the holster, rotate the gun to point down-range or forward, and start to drive out while bringing your support hand in to finish the grip. There is a saying, "Fast is slow, slow is fast." This means if you try to hurry, you will actually be slower by correcting errors. Practice it slowly, getting the feel for the sequence of movement, and you will get faster.

Figure 28 - Drawing 1

Notice as I start to draw my gun, my opposite hand is up in the stay back or stop posture. It is also up to deflect a blow and to protect my face. Just remember, if you shoot one handed, make sure your opposite hand is behind the muzzle just in case.

Figure 29 - Drawing 2

Continuing the draw stroke straight up to clear, and then begin to rotate and bring in your support hand.

Figure 30 - Drawing 3

Figure 31 - Drawing 4

Notice the strong hand is high on the backstrap, and the weak hand fingers are wrapped knuckle over knuckle of the strong hand. There is tension in the arms, and the posture is leaning slightly forward for balance and to help manage recoil.

One of my favorite things to do is speed shoot. I shoot at a range that has an electronic carrier system, so I can send my target out to twenty-five feet, hit home, and it will travel back to me. I will generally use unsighted fire, aiming

Figure 32 - Drawing 5

for center chest, and just dump the magazine as fast as I can before the target gets to me. With practice, I've been able to do this, reload, and empty the second magazine. Yes, it is a little expensive because you go through the ammo really fast, but it is also a lot of fun. I like to save it for the end of a session, shoot off whatever is left over, and also work on my unsighted fire at the same time. What is unsighted fire, sometimes called point shooting? You are not using your sights, you are using your natural sight alignment. Your body knows, especially after you've been shooting a while, where your gun is pointed. If you don't need that precise shot, you can, with practice, learn to use your natural point of aim and dump all your rounds in a center chest area without using your sights. This is a technique I also use with students once I'm assured that they are competent. I will let them dump a magazine into an advancing target. The common reaction is, "That was cool!" and they want to do it again.

In the worst cast situation, you may need a fresh magazine. You you should always carry a spare or two just in case. I say worst case, in my situation, as my gun holds fifteen rounds in the magazine and one in the chamber, for a total of sixteen shots. If I need more than that, I'm really in trouble. But your firearm could jam, the magazine release might have been pushed in a struggle for the gun, or you simply went dry. For whatever reason, you need a fresh magazine. Bring the gun back into your workspace—the area where we open the stubborn jar of peanut butter. With your strong hand, press the magazine release button, and let the magazine fall away freely. With your other hand, you are reaching for your fresh magazine, aligning your index finger along the front edge of the magazine, and inserting the magazine into the well on your gun. Once you have seated your magazine, roll your hand up and over the slide, grasp firmly in an overhand position and rack the slide, pull all the way back, and let it fly. Some people like to press the slide stop. While pressing the slide stop button to release the slide may look cool—we've all seen someone do it—there are two potential problems. First, when you rack the slide you will notice that it pulls back an additional 1/8 to 1/4 inch and fully compresses the recoil spring, allowing the gun to do what it was designed to do. Without that extra compression, the gun may not cycle fully, and the round may not load, making the gun a pretty paperweight until you can clear it. Secondly, the slide stop is just that—it is designed to stop the slide. It is also a small piece of metal that could break over time and would be expensive to have replaced. I know me, and I am quite familiar with Murphy's Law. If I did that, it would break when I needed it most.

A key point when reloading your gun: DO NOT LOOK AT THE GUN! You've practiced—your finger knows where your hand is. Do not watch your reload, as it will slow you down and possibly cause you to have trouble finding the magazine well. Don't believe me? Have several cups of coffee, get stuck in traffic, finally arrive home, and then try to put your key in the door while you are doing the pee-pee dance. If you watch, you will be all over the place. If you look away, it goes right in.

There is some debate in the shooting community about retaining your magazines in a defensive situation. I've practiced catching a mag between my ring and pinky finger while the spare is ready to load held by my thumb and index finger, but it is tough. This is situation dependent. If you are in a normal urban environment in a defensive encounter, it is probably best to let it drop. If you are in an isolated environment with access to more ammunition but not magazines, you may want to keep it. If you think you will want to keep your mag, you need to practice, practice, practice your reload and then driving out to shoot with one hand while the other is storing the empty mag. If your shirt is tucked in, you can drop it inside your collar or shove it in a pocket or waistband. I do not suggest trying to reinsert it into your magazine holder. What happens if you have a double mag holder and you go dry a second time, reach for the magazine, and pull the empty by mistake? You lose valuable seconds that you probably need to defend yourself. Not only that, but that is a small hole to find and insert something into. Better to shove the magazine somewhere out of the way and worry about it later. This philosophy actually came to the forefront after Hurricane Katrina. Police officers in New Orleans were dropping their magazines into murky water and then not able to find them later, eventually running low on magazines. Consider where you are and what you have access to.

Generally, it is wise to let it drop to the table, floor, or ground. Worry about it later. Practice this when you go to the range so you aren't trying to catch it out of habit in a defensive situation. Are you thinking that magazines are expensive, and you don't want to break one by letting it fall to the ground? Think about this. They are not that fragile, and if it breaks, there was probably a defect. Is that what you want in your gun? When you are trusting your life to your gun, your magazine is a critical component. You need to trust it will work as designed. If you drop it on the ground, just be sure to wipe it down before you put it away to get the dust off.

When Nothing Works

You are doing everything right, practicing, trying the various techniques, but you aren't hitting your target where you want to? Go back to your fundamentals. Check your stance;

start back with the isosceles position until you get comfortable again. Check your grip—if you are shooting a semiautomatic, is your support hand high on the backstrap? Are your fingers wrapped around the front strap and touching the underside of the trigger guard? Is your thumb laying along the frame and pointed forward? On your strong hand, are the heels of your hands tight together with the strong thumb laying on top of your support thumb? Are your strong fingers wrapped over your support fingers, knuckle over knuckle? Is your trigger finger using just the center of the first pad of your finger? Do you have a good sight picture and alignment? If you are shooting at the half-inch dot, you probably won't see it because it is covered by the front post. Are you using good trigger control? Are you easing the trigger straight to the rear to a surprise break? Are you riding the trigger back to the reset and keeping contact with the trigger? What is your target telling you? Everything you need to know.

The following guidelines apply to right-handed shooters, but you can simply reverse them if you are left-hand dominant.

- Are your shots pretty much left of center? Try a little more finger on the trigger.
- Are your shots to the right of center? Try a little less finger on the trigger.
- Shots moving up? Are you heeling, or putting too much pressure on the butt of the gun with your hand?
- Shots moving down? Are you anticipating the shot and dropping the muzzle?
- Shots all over the place? Are you jerking or slapping your trigger?

It is rarely just one thing, but knowing how to read your target can help immensely at diagnosing and correcting any issues. Start shooting close up, maybe at eight to ten feet. This can help you get your confidence back, and then slowly work the target out a few feet at a time.

Another common mistake, not just for new shooters, is poor trigger control. Using just the front tip of your index finger, between the end and the first joint, ease the trigger straight back to a surprise break—that means you are not anticipating the gun firing. Bang, now hold the trigger back for a fraction of a second, and then ease it out until it resets. For most guns there is a click you can feel. Some guns have a double click, and a few do not have a perceptible click at all, but you will learn how far is far enough for your gun. You do not need to remove your finger from the trigger or jerk it. Use smooth, steady pressure and release to the reset.

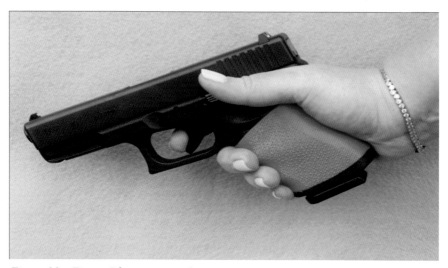

Figure 33 - Finger Placement on the Trigger

When all else fails, have an experienced shooter watch you for a few minutes. I was having a really bad shooting day, so I asked an experienced friend to watch me. It took three shots for him to tell me my shoulders were up around my ears. I was tense and raising my shoulders without realizing it, and it was impacting my aim. I dropped my shoulders and was back to shooting like I normally do. You can have an error in posture and not be aware of it. Don't be afraid to ask someone to watch you for a minute and see if they can spot the problem.

8. Challenge Your Aggressor!

If someone is advancing on you, look at them, make eye contact, and let them know you see them. Sometimes that, along with an erect, no-nonsense, and posture, can deter an attacker. Don't be afraid to say "STOP," "STAY BACK," or whatever words work for you in a voice that says, "I MEAN IT!" A hand up in the classic stop palm toward the person also sends a message of I see you, you are getting too close, and you need to back off.

Figure 34 - STOP

If it is someone who wasn't paying attention and wandered too close, you may just get their attention and an apology. If it is someone with ill intent, you will really get their notice. In the worst case you may be embarrassed but safe. In the best case you will have stopped an attack before it could happen.

Someone told a story in a class I attended of how their firearm stopped an attack without her ever having to touch the gun. She was in a parking lot and spotted two men coming toward her from different angles, making eye contact with each other, and something just felt off. She was armed but made no overt move for her gun—just her posture and taking notice of them caused one to look at the other and give a slight shake of the head, signaling that this was not a woman they wanted to mess with. This made me wonder how many times someone might have looked at me but noticed that I was alert and ready. I'll never know, but I will continue to keep looking.

9. Concealment or Cover?

What is the difference, and why do I care? Concealment hides you while cover protects you. A drapery may hide you, but it won't stop a bullet. A steel beam may hide you, and it will stop a bullet. So given a choice, which would you prefer? Cover! But what if you still need to shoot? The idea is to expose as little of your body as possible. You don't want to pop your head out and then back out looking for the assailant. Ever play Whack-a-Mole? If they saw you the first time, they know where you are likely to pop out next and will probably be waiting for you to do it.

Shuffling slightly toward the open side, you want to lean your body out to see around the barrier but expose as little of yourself as possible. You are also leading with your gun, which is a couple inches back from the barrier so you don't get caught on it or impede the slide in any way. This is dangerous stuff in the real world, which is why I encourage you to let police clear your house instead of trying to do it yourself if you come home and the door is open. But if you are trapped, you need to be able to defend yourself. It is called pie-ing, taking a little slice at a time and minimizing your exposure.

Figure 35 - Pie-ing 1

Figure 36 - Pie-ing 2

This can be practiced at home with a blue gun and at many ranges. Some will let you hang a piece of cardboard to act as a barrier, and some will let you stand a folding table vertically, although a friend who lets students do this at his range has an embarrassing number of holes in the side of the table. I have a tall narrow box that had been shipped to me. I used duct tape to secure a brick in the bottom and fashioned a handle at the top to make it easier to carry. This allows me to place the box on the shooting table in the booth and use it as my barrier. Get creative and have fun, but know you are learning skills that may save your life.

If you are training at home, have a friend or partner take photos of you as you are leaning out. It may come as a shock how much of you is exposed. This is a great tool for learning how much is too much and what is just right.

10. Concealed Carry and Defensive Tactics When You Are Expecting

Being pregnant can be an amazing time in your life. It can also be a challenging time—hormones, physical changes, swollen ankles, and a modified center of gravity all contribute to the challenges presented by your ever-changing body. You may also feel more vulnerable the further along you are, as your tummy grows and you morph from a normal pace to more of a waddle. Just as it is fine to tell people to step back and not touch your belly—what is with that anyway, it is your body—you need to increase your situational awareness to give yourself additional time to respond to a threat. You may not be as agile or quick as you were before.

I would never encourage a pregnant women to go to the range and shoot nor would I encourage her to do more than a minimal amount of gun handling. You do not want to take in lead and chemical residue, and you don't want to expose your baby to the excess noise of the range. That is just my opinion, and I would encourage you to talk with your doctor if you have any questions about the risks.

If you choose to carry a gun for self-defense when you are expecting, how do you do it? The bigger you get, the fewer options you have based on access and mobility. How could you use a thigh band when you can't remember what your thighs look like, let alone reach them? It's the same with an ankle holster when you can't see your feet. In the waistband may not work because a belt is pretty challenging. Even a Flashbang could be a problem in later pregnancy because you have to go around the beachball on the front of your body to get to it. No offense intended here—when I was pregnant, I could just about rest a plate on my tummy while standing, which was actually pretty convenient since I couldn't stop eating.

What's a pregnant woman to do? Consider a belly band. They are stretchy, like an oversized ACE bandage, with a Velcro attachment and pockets for the gun and spare magazine. You can adjust it to wear much like a pregnancy belt, so it rides under the front of your baby bump and higher on the sides to give good concealment and access to your gun. This can work with a variety of outfits as long as you aren't wearing something skintight. So what if you are wearing a dress and have to flash your attacker? It can be worn on the outside of skirts or slacks and be covered by your top. Then if the worst happens, you have your firearm and can defend yourself if you have to.

But, you may ask, if I can't go to the range, how do I practice this carry method and shooting? Great question! Training aids! Practice with a blue gun, get used to drawing and aiming, and you can watch yourself in the mirror until you are comfortable. Or you can practice with a SIRT gun. Whatever method you use, do practice. Not only is this probably a different carry method than you are used to, you have a new body shape to work around. Practicing is not a one and done in this case. As you continue to grow and change, you need to continue to practice to be comfortable with accessing and deploying your gun. Don't let yourself get frustrated as you learn the new method. I hope you never have to use it, but if you do, won't you be glad you are prepared?

I encourage you to have someone you trust take care of loading, unloading, and periodic cleaning of your gun so you aren't exposed to the lead and chemicals. You want to minimize your handling to holstering and drawing.

So, you have a belly band and you have practiced drawing and aiming with a blue gun or a SIRT. You are comfortable that you can accomplish this successfully. What about the risk to the baby? If you are in a defensive situation, the risk is likely less than the risk from the attack you are trying to stop. Additionally, statistics tell us the average is one to three shots fired in a defensive encounter, so the exposure is minimal. Of course, your situational awareness is heightened, and your safety circle may be pushed out beyond the twenty-one-foot range to allow you more time to recognize and respond.

Many of the unarmed tactics addressed earlier are useful, especially the noisy ones. It may be a lot harder for you to have a physical tussle with an attacker, especially the arm lock and follow through since your balance has shifted. However, you can still throw a mean heel of the hand punch to the nose or underneath the jaw or an elbow thrust into a belly or chest. At this point, you are fighting for two. Do what you need to do to protect yourself and get the attacker off of you while making as much noise as possible since it will be harder for you to run away quickly. You want to attract attention and you want people to come. This will be a big factor in the success of your self-defense.

Enjoy this magical time in your life, but be prepared. Some attackers will see you as an easier target because of your size and walk, especially in later pregnancy when you can't stand up straight. Counter this with a no-nonsense attitude, an alert gaze, and an awareness of your surroundings. Project confidence—let them see that you are proud of your shape, and you are not an easy target.

11. Weapon Retention

NOTE: These are last resort techniques. Everything else has failed, and you are in imminent danger and fighting for your life.

One of the keys to a successful defense is not losing your gun. Although, if you do, remember that the grappling will often knock it out of battery, so the bad guy will not only be admiring his new gun but will be trying to figure out how to clear it . . . while you are running away!

I always recommend bringing the gun into High Compressed Ready when you aren't shooting. There are a couple of reasons. If you are extended out, it is a lot easier for someone to grab your gun, and you are not strong in the position. If they try to grab it while it is close to the chest . . . you have a better chance of keeping it.

There are a few traditional methods that are surprisingly effective, and you can try them with a partner and a blue gun, not a real gun. First, if you are facing your attacker and they make a grab, you can lunge forward and then jerk back, probably throwing him off balance and retaining your firearm. Kathy Jackson, aka The Cornered Cat, refers to this as Push Me Pull You.

Figure 37 - Gun Grab

Figure 38 - Push Pull

A second technique is to jerk the gun in a C movement, often breaking the grip and freeing yourself. Third is the J movement. Jerk the gun in the shape of a J, and it is very hard for the attacker to hang on. Both of these are extremely effective, especially if you are jerking the gun between his thumb and index finger.

Once you have done this, hopefully he is off balance, and you can run away. Remember to do a tap rack to clear your gun as you are running just in case. (A tap rack is the movement of tapping your magazine to ensure it is properly engaged and will feed properly. Then cocking the slide of the firearm so any misfired rounds will eject and clear your chamber for the next round.) If the worst happens and he gets your gun, run anyway. It is very hard to hit a moving target—ask

Figure 39 - Retention Drill 1

Figure 40 - Retention Drill 2

any hunter. Your odds are better getting out than staying to fight a now armed assailant.

Another aspect of handgun retention is when the bad guy has the gun pointed at you. You want to get it off you, take it away if at all possible, and then get away.

One possibility if confronted straight on, especially if the aggressor is holding the gun in one hand, is to use the hand closest to the gun and push outward against the inside of his wrist, which takes the muzzle off of you. Then stepping forward, use your other arm to wrap around his arm, essentially locking his elbow and keeping him from bending his arm. Expect a moment of surprise after which he will probably be struggling. You are in very close contact, but you are fighting for your life. Next, grab the top of the gun with the hand you used to push his arm out

Figure 41 - Push Off

and rotate it away from you hard. If his finger is in the trigger guard, it will likely break. This gives you a chance to grab the gun and shove into him will your full weight to push him further off balance, which will hopefully make him fall. Then you can either use the gun as a club on the back of the head or if he is already down . . . run, doing a tap rack as you go. This is much harder if the attacker has both hands

Figure 42 - Arm Lock

Figure 43 - Follow Through

on the gun, but it is still doable.

The number one key for all of these techniques is speed. You act compliant and then . . . surprise! The only way to get fast is to practice, practice, practice. Start slow, and make sure your partner **never** puts his finger in the trigger guard of the blue gun. I wouldn't want to explain to the ER doctor that I was wrestling a gun away and that is how my partner broke their finger.

Get the gun away or keep a hold of yours and get away. If you are pushing into them, follow through to knock them down and RUN! Get away—don't stay and continue to fight, don't shoot them if they are no longer an immediate threat (the law takes a very dim view of that), and get away.

What about a knife-wielding assailant? The technique to disarm someone with a gun is also effective with a knife but with additional risk to you of getting cut. Once you have it, you can hang on to it or throw it hard so he can't easily get it and come after you. Personally, I would throw it as far away from me as I could so I didn't risk him knocking me down and getting it back. The time he spends looking for his knife is my chance to run away.

12. Do Not Try This at Home

I f you are in a life or death situation, you are willing to take some risks that you might not be willing to do in a training environment. This is one of those risks. If someone has a semiautomatic gun and you are to the side of the gun—not directly facing them, as if the gun were being aimed at another person—you can catch them by surprise by placing your hand over the slide and cup your hand over the ejection port. The gun can still be fired once. However, the brass won't be able to eject, and it will cause a hard malfunction; this usually takes ejecting the magazine to clear—a tap rack wouldn't do it—leaving a lot of time to run before the gun is ready to go again. This is inherently dangerous and very scary. I do not recommend trying this unless your life depends on it. Research shows it can be done safely, but unless you have to, why take the risk? Yes, I did it for the photos after much research, but I did it the first time with a leather glove to prove to myself it was safe—like that would have protected me much—and the second time bare-handed. Yes, it scared the jeepers out of the entire crew (myself included) and no one else wanted to try it. But if you have to, if your life depends on it . . . it works. There was no burn, no slide bite, just a hard malfunction. Now that I've done it twice, would I consider doing it again for demonstration? Probably not, I've already earned my BA points for this one, and there is always a risk. This is not a parlor trick, and I don't recommend doing it unless you have to.

This happens very fast. I didn't really feel the slide move, but if you look at the close-up photo, you can see that the slide is back, and the barrel is exposed. I don't know that I was able to put enough drag on the slide to make a difference, but it was blocking the brass.

Figure 44 - Slide Grab

13. Physical Confrontation

NOTE: These are last resort techniques. Everything else has failed, and you are in imminent danger and fighting for your life.

Again, this is to be avoided if at all possible. The risks of getting hurt in a physical confrontation are very real, and if you can be somewhere else, that is your best defense. If you must fight back, the following are some simple techniques that may buy you time to escape. Anytime you strike, you MUST be decisive and put everything you have into it. You cannot be tentative or it will be ineffective, and you are telling the attacker that you won't fight. Also, it is important to remember if you do strike, you can't take it back and ask for a do over. If you strike first, be sure you aren't escalating a situation that wasn't physical into one that is.

First, the three places we are strongest are the heel of the hand, the outside of the forearm, and the elbow. Holding your fingers back out of the way, you can strike hard and fast with the heel of your hand. Face to face, you can thrust your hand up under the assailant's chin, knocking his teeth together and sending his head back, effectively ringing his bell for at least a few seconds and giving you time to run away or attract help.

The side of the forearm can be effective against the side of the neck to push him off balance. You hit him hard enough, it may momentarily disrupt the blood flow to his brain and leave him dazed to give you a chance to escape.

The elbow, especially if he is behind you, is very effective to the ribs, solar plexus, and abdomen. Then when he doubles over, give him a good shove to knock him down and then make your escape.

Figure 45 - Heel of the Hand to the Jaw

Figure 46 - Elbow Strike

Figure 47 - Forearm to the Neck

The face rake is essentially a clawed hand into the eyes and pull down. Yes, it sounds disgusting, but I prefer that to being raped or murdered.

Figure 48 - Face Rake

If he grabs your arm to pull you, splay your fingers out tight. This gives you more strength to resist. This one is surprisingly easy and very effective.

Figure 49 - Splayed Hand

If he grabs your clothing to pull you, grab a handful of clothing right below where he is handing on, taking the slack out of the fabric, and drop fast just a few inches—not enough to put you off balance. This will free you, leaving him holding air, and give you a chance to respond or run.

If he is running toward you with his arm reaching, you can step to the side, grab his arm, and use his momentum to help propel him farther away from you.

Many men will force a woman to the ground while thinking it makes her more vulnerable. Don't be fooled. A sideways kick to the shin can temporarily disable him. Why sideways?

If you kick with your foot on the same vertical plane as his leg, chances are good you will deliver a glancing blow, but if your foot is turned like the cross on a T, you will impart more force and more contact. A key point here is **this is why I don't encourage small-of-the-back carry**! If you get knocked to the ground, there is a high risk you will land on your back and on your gun. That alone could cause serious injury, but it also makes it difficult to access your gun.

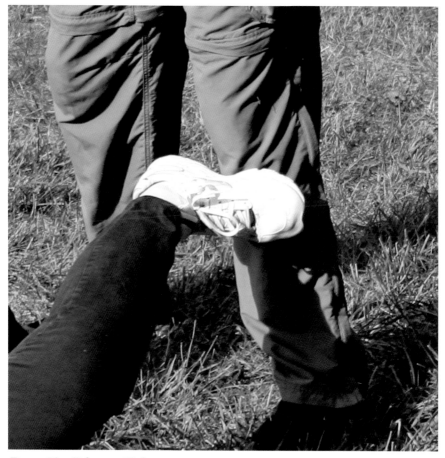

Figure 50 - Sideways Kick

Figure 51 - Fighting on Your Back

Make no mistake, if he makes contact with you, it will hurt. Adrenaline may help ease the pain, but if you have never been hit, it will be quite a shock. Do not let this deter you. You are worth protecting; your safety is important and **no one** has the right to take that away from you. When I teach basic personal safety classes, I offer my students the opportunity not only to hit the pad while I hold it but to hold that pad as I gradually increase the force behind the blows to help them come to terms with taking a hit. While holding a pad and having someone you trust hit it isn't the same as being cold cocked by a stranger, it does go a long way to reduce the initial shock.

Figure 52 - Muy Thai Pad 1

Figure 53 - Muy Thai Pad 2

Many women think that going for the groin is a good bet. Remember, little boys quickly learn to protect this area, and grown men haven't forgotten. Better to hit him where he isn't expecting it. Go for the abdomen, the solar plexis, face, and even the top of the foot. Then if you get him stunned and have a good shot, go for it, but that isn't always where you want to start.

Before you hit, be sure that the situation has escalated to the point where physical contact is absolutely necessary. If you are approached and you punch the guy and then he grabs you and wrestles you to the ground, you can't say, "I'm sorry, I didn't mean to hit you, it was an accident, can we have a do over?" You are committed. Show your attacker the same mercy they are showing you, but do not go beyond what you have to do to get away. That becomes a matter for the legal system. However, if it does get physical, do whatever it takes!

14. Teaching Your Kids to Defend Themselves

If your kids are old enough to walk, they are old enough to learn some basic defense. Techniques will vary by age, but they can learn from you to be confident and protect themselves. The hard part as the parent is to make it memorable but not too scary. There is a fine line there, and only you can judge how much your child can handle.

For the little ones, teach them the importance of not wandering off in a store. Make it about you being frightened if you can't see them, not about what could happen to them. The old rule about not talking to strangers is a good one. However, if you do get separated, they should know to go to a clerk or police officer for help. Also, teach them to yell loudly "STRANGER" if someone they do not know tries to touch them or pick them up. No adult needs to touch a child they don't know unless the child is injured and they are helping to get a parent. A child who is scooped up and is screaming, "STRANGER, YOU AREN'T MY MOM!" is not likely to get far without someone intervening and getting your attention. A common ploy at a park is a lost dog or a box full of kittens in a car. Someone may approach your child and ask them to help look for the lost dog or ask if they want to come see the kittens. Instruct your child to tell whoever approaches them that they need to get mom first and then they will come see. If it is legitimate, be prepared to take home a new kitten, if not the stranger is likely to vanish before you can get there.

Code words are important for family security. These are secret words that only you and your children know. If someone attempts to pick them up from day care, school, or walking home and they don't have the code word, the child knows not to go with them, to yell, and to run away.

As your child gets older and is able to go farther on their own, it is important that they learn situational awareness. You can make a game of it so it's not as scary by having them point out what they see and tell you if it belongs. This helps them distinguish what should be there from what shouldn't. This is a potentially valuable skill even for the little ones.

As the child gets older, they can carry a personal alarm on their backpack. They can begin to learn basic punches, such as the heel of the hand under the chin. They also need to learn where to go and where not to. Stick to main streets and roads, and don't cut through vacant lots, constructions sites, or wooded areas.

If your child can walk, they need to start to learn about protecting themselves. Your job is to keep them safe. As they become teenagers, many of the unarmed techniques here will work for them. First and foremost is that they understand that these are important things to learn but not to talk about. Never share the family's secret word, and understand that just because someone approaches them doesn't make that person dangerous, but they need to be wary. We want our kids to be safe but to be comfortable going out of the house. If they know how to respond, you can worry less, too.

You might want to consider making a contract with your teen and they with you. It may seem odd, but their safety is the most important thing to you, and they need to trust you. Sample contracts follow. You don't have to use these exact words, but there are some key points.

FOR THE PARENT

I pledge to come and get you at any time, day or night, wherever you are if you feel you are not safe or for any reason. I promise to come when you need me and bring you home. I will not ask questions beyond if you need anything, such as medical care, food, or warmth. I promise to hug you and love you and not yell or lecture but simply to make you safe. I will hold my questions and concerns until the next day when you and I are calm. I promise to listen, not to judge, and to remember that you were smart and trusting in calling me for help.

FOR THE TEEN

I pledge to call you to come get me if ever I feel unsafe or I am hurt or scared. I will not ride in a car with friends who are drinking or on drugs; I will ask you to come get me. I will not stay where I don't feel safe, and I will trust you to make me safe and not judge. I am young and I will make mistakes, but I trust you to love me, help me, and not lecture when I ask for help. I trust you to come for me anytime, anywhere when I need you.

Do you notice the themes? Trust, love, safety. It goes both ways. You need to trust your child to call you for help, and they need to trust you will be there with no lecture, no questions, but to get them to a safe place, hug them, love them, and protect them. Only if you trust each other will you give them the freedom they need to grow and thrive. Kids make mistakes. I did, and you probably did, too. I survived my youth, as did you. Help your child grow to adulthood with the ability to look back and realize they, too, survived the choices they made.

Write out your pledges and sign them. Keep them safe or carry them with you. Let your children know you will protect them, you will come get them, and you will love them no matter what.

15. Rape – An Act of Violence

ape is about violence, not sex. If you are a victim, it is critical to get counseling, to understand that you didn't ask for it no matter what he says, and that it isn't about sex—it is about violence, aggression, and domination. Even a brush with a sexually based attack can leave you devastated and going through the stages of denial and shock. In the beginning of this book I talked about being grabbed while hiking in the mountains alone. Even though I was not injured, I was assaulted, and I really struggled with that. Looking back, I had the classic response of wanting a hot shower and feeling dirty, as if I would never get clean again. That was just from a secondary touch. I cannot imagine the devastation of something more serious.

The Rape, Abuse and Incest National Network (RAINN) published some eye-opening statistics on their website. These numbers are provided by the US Department of Justice.

- Approximately ⅔ of rapes are committed by someone the victim knows.
- 73% of sexual assaults are perpetrated by a non-stranger.

- 38% of rapists are a friend or acquaintance.
- 28% are an intimate.
- 7% are a relative.
- 40% occur in the victim's home.
- 20% occur in the home of a friend, neighbor, or relative.
- 1 in 12 occur in a parking garage.
- 43% of rapes occur between 6 pm and midnight.

Wow, those are pretty scary odds when you look at the raw numbers. Does this mean an attack is inevitable, you just don't know when? NO! We can't always stop bad things from happening, but there is a lot we can do to minimize our risk.

Acquaintance and date rapes are the largest percentage. Do you really know who you are letting into your home? You had a great first date with someone you met online, you feel a connection, you've emailed, talked, and finally met for dinner. It was a magical night, and suddenly you don't want it to end. But being a smart, savvy woman, you met him at the restaurant for the first date. What do you do when he encourages you to invite him back to your place? If the first date was awesome, he will understand that you want to take it slow, get to know him, and can't wait for the second date. If he is a predator in Mr. Right's clothing, he won't call for the second date. What if you end your date with a nice kiss in the parking lot and drive home? Minutes later you hear a knock at the door. Looking out, do you see your date? How did he know? He most likely followed you, and you should not let him in! You can tell him through the door that you had a great time, but you have to get up early. Have your phone handy and ready to dial 911 if he doesn't leave. Someone who will do this is **not** someone you want a second date with. He crossed the line from date to potential stalker or rapist by following you home.

Trust your instincts. I once invited a contractor who was doing some work on my home to dinner. He was funny and nice, and I wanted to get to know him better. He was already spending a lot of time in my home, so I decided to cook dinner for us. Afterward, we were sitting on the couch and he got . . . amorous. I told him I wasn't ready for that and I wanted to get to know him. Then he got a little grabby. At that point, I grabbed his hand by the thumb, twisting it back hard enough to pull off me and make him wince while simultaneously standing up. (It's amazing how much more forceful you seem when you are standing.) I told him that I had said NO, and now it was time to leave—and that he was no longer welcome in my home, and someone else from his company would need to finish the work. I'm not unaware and not stupid, but I have been fooled more than once by the predator, or the overly randy contractor. That point is, you can miss the early signs, but once you know, react. Get him out. Don't dismiss the tingling on the back of your neck because you don't want to risk offending him. If he is offended that you protected your-self when you felt uncomfortable, then you don't want him around anyway.

Be leery of the ploy to get close to you. The cute neighbor who offers to carry your groceries to your apartment door— is he a gentleman or a potential rapist? It's hard to know, so it's probably better to carry your own groceries. You hear someone call you over to help with something, maybe in a parking lot near a van . . . do you go? It is a risk, and you need to trust your instincts. Are there a lot of people around? Is this someone you know well? Often it is safe, but sometimes it isn't, and it can be hard to tell until it is too late. It is sad, but it might be best to say, "I'm sorry, I can't help you," and keep going.

The majority of acquaintance rapists used physical assault and violence to subdue or intimidate their victims. They did not use a weapon. Only you know what you can do, and you have to decide how far along is the assault? Still in the early stage where you can wriggle out and demand he leave? Or have you been enjoying some serious kissing time, and suddenly he goes further than you are prepared for? Start with firmly saying "NO" or "STOP." For the man caught up in the moment, that may be enough to break the spell. If so, get him out and talk about it later. For the man who isn't prepared to stop, remember it doesn't matter if you were intimate before or if you had just spent the last three hours snuggling and kissing on the couch. It is your choice, and NO means NO! If you can and have to, physically resist and do what you need to. Push and roll to knock him off balance, hit him with anything in reach—a book, a lamp, something that is hard and weighty that will get his attention. Be prepared to be called some rude names, but it's ok. The words don't matter, you do.

If the worst happens, your first priority is survival. Do whatever you have to do to make it through. Then call the police or go to the emergency room. Resist the temptation to take that hot shower and wash away evidence. Even if you opt not to file a complaint with the police, the emergency room can collect the evidence, and it is there if you decide the next day that you do want to report it. Also, they can check you for injuries, test for diseases, and if you want, possibly provide you with emergency contraception. Birth control may be the last thing on your mind following a rape, but pregnancy is a risk.

Lastly, no matter what, if you are the victim of an attempted assault, rape, or violent stranger rape . . . seek out a counselor who specializes in dealing with rape victims. The doctors at the ER or the police can probably refer you. You can visit www.RAINN.org to find help. Talk to someone. Do not suffer this in silence—it will haunt you. Don't let yourself be victimized by the memories, talk to someone who can help. If you were victimized using a date rape drug, you may not have memories of the assault, but your body knows. Get help to cope.

Remember the earlier discussion on situational awareness and pay attention. Your awareness and intuition are your best defense.

16. Out with My Family

This is a terrifying situation. You are out with your family and suddenly find yourself facing a threat. It is scary, and your first priority is to protect your loved ones . . . what do you do? You practice, so you and they know what to do. My former husband used to jokingly call me his bodyguard because I would be armed and he wasn't a shooter. One day I asked him, "What would you do if we were confronted by a mugger?" At first he said he would step forward and push me back. After some discussion, he rethought that, since I'm the one with the gun. His next response was even more frightening. He said, "I would get behind you." Why is that so scary? Where would my attention be? If I were shot, there is a good chance if he were right behind me, he would be, too. Would I be able to move freely, if I were not sure where he was? Would I trip over him? We finally worked out a signal. He could be manly and handle panhandlers or people who were more annoying than dangerous, but at the first sign of a serious danger—and we had a code word—he was to move away from me on a diagonal. That took him to either side, preferably to cover, and out of the line of fire, allowing me to focus on the threat and not worry about him. With a little luck, it would also confuse the jeepers out of a mugger—seeing the man run away while he's left being faced down by a woman. In my case, I look pretty harmless . . . until you see me throw a punch or pull a gun, then I can be pretty scary.

Figure 54 - Running Away on the Diagonal

I've interviewed people who do drills with their children when they are out walking. The parent will suddenly shout the code word, and the kids scatter away from the parent and to concealment if not cover. They don't come back until they hear the right all-clear code word that the family has established. This had become a game for them on family walks, but it also teaches the kids to get out of the way to a safe place and to stay hidden until called out by a parent or police officer. Why not? We do fire drills, tornado drills, hurricane drills, and earthquake drills to teach our kids what to do in an emergency. This is a bit like a safety version of hide and seek.

Tips for parents: Ensure your child doesn't share the code words—they're a family secret. You can practice the drills without scaring them by making it a game, but let them know it is important. They will be able to tell the difference between a drill and a real situation, but you want them to react, not stop and panic. The only way to ensure that is to practice.

This is also a good time to remind the children that if someone approaches them that they don't know, yell "**stranger**" as loud as they can. If someone is trying to drag them off, they can yell, "Stranger, you aren't my mom!" Almost every adult within earshot will come running at the sound of a child in distress.

17. In with the Family

Your home is your safe haven, your castle, and nothing bad can happen within its walls, right? **Wrong**! Things can and do go wrong at home during both night and day time.

Statistics are funny things. The same numbers can be manipulated to prove a theory or disprove a theory. So with that in mind, statistics show that many home invasions occur between 10 am and 4 pm. Why? Most people are at work! Houses are empty.

There is something about broad daylight that gives us a sense of comfort that we don't have when it is dark. It isn't as scary when the sun is shining and the sky is blue. Should it be? In a word, yes! Bad things happen in the daylight, too. Think about your home on a warm fall day with the doors open to catch the fresh air. You may be at the computer, in the kitchen, or even dozing on the sofa and all of a sudden . . . crash! Someone comes through the door. Obviously they know someone is home because the house is opened up, and they come in anyway. These are the most dangerous kinds of criminals—the ones who don't care. Will they tie you up and rob the house or worse? Are you prepared? Are you carrying your gun on you in the house? You'd be surprised how many people don't. Do you at least have quick access to a firearm? Have you thought about how to gather up the family or even get yourself to a safer place?

A couple years ago a local community was victimized by a group of teens who broke into occupied homes, tied up the families, and robbed the homes. Luckily no one was killed before the police caught these thugs. I found out because I was invited to teach a basic firearms class for members of the community in someone's home. (That was the first of what we now call Home Training Parties that I've conducted.) We had a lot of fun and used a nearby range for the shooting portion. But what was most important was that these folks were afraid. We are supposed to be safe in our homes—they are where we relax, where we sleep, and where we let our guard down. Even if they weren't victims of this gang directly, they were victims of the terror that was spread by them. Several of these folks had guns but had never gotten around to learning to shoot. That may be one of the scariest aspects. If you have a gun and haven't learned to shoot—well, you probably wouldn't be reading this book, but you are also placing yourself and your family in even more danger by providing a weapon for your attacker that they may not have brought with them.

This is something to think about. It isn't paranoid to be armed at home, it's smart.

18. One of the Most Dangerous Places to Be

O f all the possibilities, what would you think would be one of the most dangerous places to be? If you guessed a parking lot, you would be right. Scan the web for stories about abductions and assaults; see how many occurred in a parking lot. People are distracted and heading to their cars. Criminals have easy access to getaway vehicles, or they can steal your car. You can be knocked down between cars and not easily seen by someone who could help. They are often noisy, so a scream might go unnoticed. Many parking lots and garages are poorly lit. With lots of hiding places, it is easy to get lost in the crowd.

Your situational awareness needs to be on full alert in a parking lot!

Are you loading children into a car? That's fine, just make sure your other doors are locked and keep an eye on your windows—use them like mirrors to see if someone is coming up behind you.

Figure 55 - Reflection in Car Window

Are you loading groceries in the back of your car? Use the cart as a barrier and keep up your scan.

Figure 56 - Shopping Cart Barrier

Don't walk out of a store and into the parking lot with your arms loaded, peeking over the top of the packages, or thinking, "I will find my keys when I get to my car." That is akin to being a walking advertisement with a flashing neon light over you to any criminal! Your keys should be IN YOUR HAND before you ever step into the parking lot. The one exception to this is if you have keyless entry, such as we find on many newer cars, where you simply have to be in the vicinity. Even then, if you have pepper spray on your key chain, it doesn't do you any good in the bottom of your purse.

Hang up the cell phone, stop texting, and pay attention. There aren't just muggers and criminals; there are distracted and sometimes frustrated drivers, especially during the holidays. Once I saw a woman who was extremely intent on her texting as she walked through a parking lot. It was clear she had no idea what was going on around her. As she got closer, I stopped my car so I wouldn't hit her, and she walked into the side of my car. She wasn't hurt, but at first she was angry— what was I doing in the street? Then she realized that she was the one being irresponsible and put away the phone as she walked off. Had I been less alert, the outcome may have been quite different. It is dangerous.

Stay alert, and don't walk too close to parked cars. If a large vehicle is parked close to yours, trust your instincts—go back in and ask a security officer to walk you to your car. Scan your safety circle, and be sure that you know what and who is around you. Better to be safe and wrong, than to be right but dead.

19. Carjacking

The Department of Justice cites an average of 49,000 carjackings every year. You can take steps to minimize your risk.

First, let's look at your circumstances. Crime statistics tell us most carjackings occur at an intersection where you are stopped or in a parking lot, such as at the mall or a grocery store. These statistics also tell us that there are usually two attackers, and they have weapons. No one likes to meekly hand over something that they've worked hard for, but remember **your car can be replaced, you can't**. However, everything changes if your child or children are in the car. Arguing or pleading for time to get your child safely out of the car is not likely to be successful, as the whole point for a carjacker is to catch you off guard, nab the car, and get away as fast as possible.

Let's look at ways to minimize your risk. At an intersection, try to avoid allowing yourself to be boxed in with nowhere to go. If you are stopped, can you see the rear tires and some pavement behind the car in front of you? If not, you are too close. In a parking lot, keep your keys in your hand, and keep all doors except the one you are

Figure 57 - Safe Distance When Stopped

using locked. Be aware of your surroundings. Are people watching you? Does something feel off? Use your windows as reflective surfaces to help you to see what is happening around you. If you have a shopping cart, position it behind you to improvise a barrier that may give you an extra second to respond if something happens. Use your safety circle, a twenty-one-foot radius around you that no one enters without you noticing them. Most people will pass harmlessly through your safety circle, but if they enter and come toward you, you want as much notice as possible. Once you are inside your car, lock your doors, keep the windows up, and get moving. This is not the time to check text messages or dig in your purse.

Another all too common tactic for carjackers is the bumper kiss. They deliberately run into the back of your car. What is the first thing most people do? Get out and check the damage. At that point, you are vulnerable; there is nothing between you and the carjackers except air. Trust your instincts. Are you in an isolated area? Turn on your flashers, and wave to the other driver to follow you to a safer location. If they take off, that is a pretty good indication that it was an attempted robbery. Resist the temptation to get out of the car if you are not in an area that feels safe to you. If the area isn't well-lit or populated, it is better to deal with the police and insurance company for minor damage than to lose your car and possibly your life. A twist on this scenario is the reverse bumper kiss, which is often accomplished by a team working in tandem. One will pull in close to you from behind at an intersection, and the car in front of you suddenly goes into reverse and, bang, backs into you. You are now wedged between two vehicles. At this point, your options are more limited. Since it is probable that this was not a mistake, you can try to accelerate to push the car away and make room, or you can start making lots of noise to attract attention.

For the remainder of this chapter, I am assuming that you have precious cargo or some very serious reason to resist, and we will look at your options. Your response will vary with the circumstances. Remember, the attacker is looking for a quick getaway. You can try hitting the gas to drive off, laying on the horn, or if you feel your life is in jeopardy, you may opt for an armed response.

Drawing and firing from inside a car presents some challenges. You need to work around your seat belt, or you need to have stashed your concealed carry gun when you first entered your car. Some opt to keep a holster or pistol sleeve, such as a Remora holster, tucked between the seats or seat and center console. Gum Creek makes an adjustable strap that clamps onto the steering column, and you can attach a simple single-clip holster to it that fits your gun. There are also holster straps that fit over the car seat so the gun rests behind your knees, but for me, I found that to be uncomfortable and difficult to access, especially when I'm wearing a skirt. And I kept snagging my stockings on it—something most men don't have to worry about.

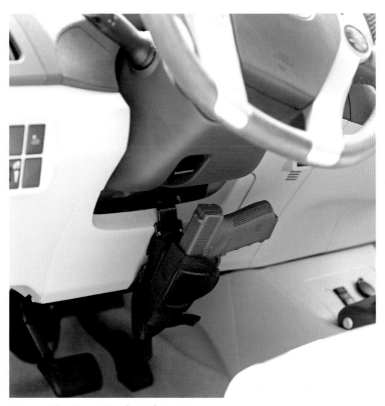

Figure 58 - Gum Creek Holster Strap

If you opt not to unholster and stow your gun, be aware of coats or outer garments that will inhibit your access. I like to push my jacket outside my seatbelt, lift my top, and tuck it in behind my gun, which leaves it more exposed. I can easily pull the shirt down before I exit the car. The three easiest carry positions for inside the vehicle when you are the driver are the right hip (if your navel is 12:00, about the 3:00 to 3:30 position), cross draw (left for those who are right-handed) appendix position, or the Flashbang bra holster. Of course, this depends on your attire and your firearm.

For the right hip, I really like the Ava from the Looper Law Enforcement—the same folks who make the Flashbang bra holsters—Pinup collection. The Ava is a hybrid that is cut lower for a woman's curvier shape and has a lovely purple suede backing that is kind to my skin. For cross draw I use a ProCarry Heavy Duty Leather holster. I've heard many people say right side appendix, but I've only found that to be workable from the passenger seat. Remember, you must position your gun so you can still get to it with the seatbelt on. You need to practice your draw so you don't get hung up in the seatbelt. This can be tricky, and I strongly encourage you to practice with a blue gun or an unloaded triple-checked firearm. Be prepared to shoot one-handed and quite possibly across your body with your arm bent. This isn't really something you can practice at most ranges. Be aware of where your left hand and arm are so they are not in the line of fire. If you are left-handed, practice one-handed shooting with your right hand, as you will have more clearance that way. Remember, once you have committed to drawing your

Figure 59 - Easy Access to Gun

Figure 60 - Aiming in the Car

Figure 61 - Shooting from Inside the Car

firearm, you are committed to the fight, and you can't easily backtrack at that point.

Can you safely shoot through auto glass? Yes. Most modern auto glass will shatter but not fall due to a thin film sandwiched between the layers of safety glass. If it does shatter, it tends to have dull edges unlike a beverage glass, so it is less likely to cause you injury. Side windows offer negligible distortion of the trajectory at close range. Can you shoot through the door? Surprisingly, yes. Hollywood fiction aside, a car door is unlikely to stop a bullet unless you happen to hit the side impact panel. It may slow it down, but the bullet will most likely penetrate the door and keep going. The body that is behind the door is more difficult to judge. You are better off aiming through the window at what you can see, but if you have no other choice, through the door can be effective. You can also shoot through the windshield. Be mindful of the steering wheel. You want to be above the steering wheel so it doesn't interfere with the gun in any way. If you had to shoot at a distance, you would have to adjust your aim for the angle of the windshield and its impact on trajectory. However, if the thief is farther away than the end of the hood of your car, why are you shooting? You probably have better options at that point, such as getting away. Ensure that you are using adequate carry ammunition. Use modern heavy bonded hollow points of 124 grain or higher. Bullet weight is measured in grains, which has nothing to do with the powder—it is the weight of the projectile.

Your best defense is situational awareness. Don't let a stranger into your safety circle without you noticing them and tracking to see if they are passing by or have evil intent. You can challenge someone who comes to close—don't worry about being polite. You are being *safe*! Twenty-one feet gives you approximately two seconds to identify a threat and react. That isn't very much time, but it is better than being completely unaware.

20. Competition Shooting

I do not shoot competitively, but I like to compete with myself. What I mean is I do not shoot competitions. It isn't my passion. For many people, it is enjoyable, stressful, and fulfilling all in one. Some people say that shooting competitively prepares you for the real world, but others argue the opposite. The bottom line for me is it can offer you a great outlet to change up your style of shooting, and it can give you a glimpse of how you will respond under pressure. There is timing, accuracy, movement, people watching . . . I would call that pressure! Some would call it FUN! But whatever helps you train is valuable.

You've been shooting a while; you're ready to move to the next level. Where do you start? A great place to start is A Girl and A Gun (AGAG) shooting league. Check them out and see if there is a chapter near you. They can help you get started training for competition, as well as having fun shooting in a safe and supportive environment with other women. No AGAG near you? Check your local range for fliers or ask the managers or range security officers—they should be able to point you in the right direction.

ISPC, USPSA, SASS, Three Gun . . . Alphabet soup? These are different types of competitions, where you can move and shoot, stand in one place and shoot, and have stationary or moving targets. You can even dress up in Old West garb, adopt a persona, and compete—for some from the back of a horse! No idea what kind of competition you might be interested in? Julie Golob, Pro Shooter and National and World Champion, wrote a great book that explains the different competitions called *SHOOT*, from Skyhorse Publishing. She is also a very nice lady and a mom.

If competition interests you, jump right in! You may not score well your first time out, but think of the experience and fun of being with like-minded shooters of all skill levels. And as I have often said, "A bad day at the range beats a good day at the office."

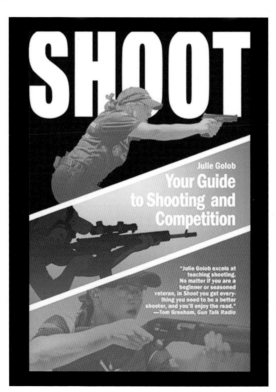

Figure 62 - SHOOT

21. Active Shooter

The Department of Homeland Security (DHS) defines an active shooter as "an individual actively engaged in killing or attempting to kill people in a confined and populated area, typically through the use of firearms." I cannot imagine a more frightening scenario. This can happen in an office, a school, a shopping mall, on the street . . . anywhere! Many of these locations have actively banned lawful concealed carry on the premises, such as the theater in Colorado where James Holmes is accused of killing twelve people and injuring seventy others in a mass shooting. The theater had banned the carrying of concealed firearms by those who had the legal right to do so. This is not a political statement but a statement of fact. Law-abiding citizens follow those rules, criminals do not. I might not use my firearm in a situation like that, but I really would like the option to do so.

You who are reading this book have an advantage. You know what a gunshot sounds like. Some of you can even tell from the sound if it is a pistol, rifle, or shotgun. Remember, an active shooter is likely to have multiple firearms, so don't make decisions based on what type of shot you heard. But you know that a gunshot in real life doesn't sound like it does in the movies—it isn't likely to be mistaken for a car backfire or other similar noise. You may be the first in your group to recognize the danger. Alert others and don't let them dissuade you—you know what you heard. They may not want to believe you at first because the thought is too horrifying to consider. Take control, get them moving, and if you can, get out of the area and away from where the shots came from to someplace safe where you can call the police.

DHS guidelines give us three options in order of preference for responding to an active shooter.

First – Run! Do not take time to grab your purse, do not pass go, do not run toward the shooter—get as far away as you can as fast as you can. Keep your hands visible; if you are exiting the building, keep your hands up and fingers spread. This lets responding authorities know you are not a danger to them. Remember, their adrenaline is high and they are going into an area with an unknown gunman trying to kill people. They want to go home to their families that night. Don't give them a reason to think you might be a threat.

Second – Hide. If you can lock the door, do so, and move heavy furniture to block the door. Silence, not put on vibrate, your cell phone. Get as far away from the door as possible and behind something that may give you cover. Do not open the door until you are certain it is the police. Bad guys lie—if you hear someone try the door and then yell, "It's the cops, open up," stay silent! If you are in a public structure, there will likely be a PA announcement letting you know what area the police are clearing.

Third (and last) resort – Prepare to Fight. Give it your all with no hesitation. Use whatever is handy. Look around where you are right now and identify three potential defensive weapons. But I'm unarmed! Wrong, look around. As I sit at my desk, I see scissors that I can stab with, I see a pencil I can jab into the face or throat, I see a lamp I can use like a club, a chair I can use to push off and create distance, and a high heeled shoe with a stiletto that can be lethal—and not just to our toes! Nearby is a fire extinguisher so you can either blast the shooter in the face with the extinguishing agent or club him with the canister. Got a coffee pot? Hot coffee in the face tends to slow someone down, as does smashing them in the face with the empty pot. These are just a few ideas; your imagination is the limit here. Think outside of the box and think what you can improvise to save yourself. Throw things, yell, and act together with others in the area to confuse the attacker. If you are coming at him from all sides, he is less likely to know where to respond.

If you are in a group and someone is panicking and unable to help, settle them as far away and crouched low as possible. You do not want them in your way when you are going after the shooter. Don't be critical, try to be patient, and calmly tell them they need to stay low and out of the way. Not everyone reacts the same way in a life or death situation, and you may never know what you will do unless you have to face one.

Try to stay calm if you are hiding, be silent, and help others who may be with you to be silent. When you get the chance to evacuate, keep your hands raised and open. If you can provide information to police about the location or number of shooters or the location of victims, do so—otherwise, let them do their jobs. If you have the opportunity to call the police, understand that they may not want to keep you on the phone, or they may ask you to leave the line open. Follow the responder's directions, and don't be upset if they take your information and hang up. Others may be calling who have information you do not.

It is a terrifying thought, some random gunman shooting people. Don't panic, be smart, and do what you need to do to protect yourself. Don't try to be a hero, help others if you can, but remember the hierarchy—run, hide, fight—in that order.

22. Care and Cleaning

Cleaning your gun is a critical aspect of caring for it. The other is proper storage. First, let's talk cleaning. I used to take a lot of teasing from other instructors. They would say things like they could eat off of my gun because I was so fanatical about cleaning it. Admittedly, I'm not that fanatical about all of my guns, but my carry gun gets cleaned EVERY time it has been fired regardless of the round count. Why? It is my carry gun. Have you ever heard of someone having a malfunction because their gun was too clean? If you have, write to me, I want to know. Conversely, I've heard stories of people who had malfunctions because their gun was dirty. OK, there is a balance, so how often should you clean? This depends partly on your gun—if you have one that can be touchy or likes a lot of lubrication, you should probably clean after each outing. If you aren't going to shoot again for a few weeks, clean. If you are going back tomorrow, you might be able to get away with not cleaning. You should know your gun well enough to judge. Some people go by round count, but I prefer the use and intent. If I only shot for an hour and plan to go to the range the next day . . . I'll probably skip the cleaning or just wipe it down.

When you clean, you are doing more than cleaning, you are visually inspecting the inside of your gun and looking for any wear patterns or unusual markings. If something doesn't look right, get it checked out by a professional. There are lot of different tools for cleaning, so use what you prefer—just remember to travel the same path down the barrel as the bullet if at all possible. Also, there are different levels of cleaning. You can do a basic disassembly of your gun, run a few patches through, wipe it down, and lube it per the manufacturer's recommendation, or you can meticulously clean. I have used long handle cotton swabs to get into small spaces, but I recently discovered something similar only with washable foam ends. (Amazon is a great resource.) Then there's no worrying about cotton threads from the swab. It is a little like detailing a car—you are getting into every groove, every well, cleaning, and drying. There is something satisfying about a well-cleaned gun.

Storage is also critical to the maintenance of your guns. I added the plural because guns are like potato chips, it's hard to stop at one. First, you want secure storage that's inaccessible to people who shouldn't have access. Do not leave your gun in the case it came in if it has egg crate foam. This retains moisture and can cause rust. If you have multiple handguns and a safe, you can get a rack to rest the guns in. Store them with the actions open, and you will be able to see that they are safe and unloaded. Desiccant, essentially a dehumidifying agent, is important. You can get containers or rechargeable units. These will help to protect your valuable firearms from moisture and rust. The Gun Vault Quick Access safe comes with a desiccant strip, so it helps protect the gun as well as securing it.

The bottom line on storage is to keep it locked, inaccessible to unauthorized persons, and minimize the impact of humidity.

23. Final Thoughts on Safety – Do Not Let These Things Happen to You!

Throughout this book, safety has been reinforced over and over through your training, your awareness, and your avoidance. What follows are some of my final thoughts on staying safe.

Alcohol and Guns – A Dangerous Combination

You probably know this, but it is so important it bears repeating. **Alcohol and guns do not mix**. Out with friends on a beautiful midsummer day at a gorgeous outdoor range with a cooler full of what? Beer? No! Water! Stay hydrated, and skip the cold brew, as it can become very dangerous very quickly.

Do you carry at home? Good idea, but it means you don't drink when you are carrying. Not even one. I know you're thinking, "One beer, I can handle that." But how many DUI arrests have said the same thing? It's not worth it. Alcohol dulls your reaction time and suppresses your good sense. It's not a good combination.

Another potential risk if you carry concealed is that some states will now allow you to enter an establishment that sells alcohol but prohibit your consumption. Don't risk jail and the loss of you carry rights because a beer sounded good. It isn't worth it!

Never Be Complacent

Never allow yourself to become complacent with your firearm. This is actually quite common among long-time shooters. They start to skip things such as triple checking, as well as visual and manual inspection, to ensure a gun is unloaded. They think, "I know it isn't loaded, I don't have to check it." They skip the safe direction. If, like me, you shoot GLOCK, you know that you must pull the trigger in order to take it apart. If you skip the safety steps and then pull the trigger, at best you may get a nasty surprise, at worst, you could lose your life. This happens more often than you would imagine. Ever see a news report of someone being shot while cleaning their gun or negligent discharge at a gun show? It happens. Do not let it happen to you!

Know your equipment. Some holsters, such as the SERPA, have a retention device that must be engaged to draw the gun. There is a famous, or infamous, video on YouTube of Tex Scibner shooting himself in the leg while trying to draw from a retention holster. He blames this, at least in part, on changing up equipment. Better to stick with what you are comfortable with, and if you introduce something new, such as a holster with retention, practice, practice, practice.

Another aspect of complacency is violating the basic three safety rules.

- Always keep the gun pointed in a safe direction.
- Always keep your finger off the trigger until you are ready to shoot.
- Always keep the gun unloaded until you are ready to use it.

You might get away with violating one of these some of the time, but at some point if you continue to do it, you will have a negligent discharge—simply meaning your gun will fire when you didn't intend it to. Why is this not an accidental discharge? Most definitions of accident include something about it being unavoidable or without cause. If you violate a safety rule and the gun discharges, it may have been unintended but it **was** avoidable. DO NOT be complacent. Resist the temptation to repeat some of the dangerous moves you see on the web, such as the guy who speed shoots and then twirls the gun on his finger before holstering like an old cowboy movie.

Emergency First Aid

Have some basic first aid training. Odds are good you will never need it, but what if you or someone near you does? Most if not all commercial indoor ranges have staff and a significant first aid kit. But if you are shooting outdoors, maybe on private property, be sure you have a basic kit with you. In the back of this book is a photo of the small kit we had for the photo shoot. The day started with a quick review of who was trained, what the kit contained, and where it would be. It is basic: gloves, tourniquet, and a pressure bandage. There isn't a photo of the bigger kit that contains a lot more to address scrapes, bee stings, sprained ankles, etc. This big kit isn't essential, but the minimum kit is for a quick response to a life-threatening injury. Better to have it and not need it than to wish you had it when the worst happens.

While we are on first aid, if you will be in an unfamiliar location, write down the address and how to call for emergency assistance. Plan to have someone head out to the main road to flag the ambulance if the area is hard to find, and let the responders know someone will be there to direct them. In some cases, the plan may be to load the injured person into a vehicle and hightail it to the closest ER. If you are really isolated, that may work, or you can call and arrange to meet first responders. The quicker you can get an injured person into the hands of well-equipped and highly trained personnel, the better their chance of survival. Personally, I cringe at the idea of moving someone who is injured because of the risk of additional injury, but you need to assess your environment. Follow the advice of the dispatcher.

BOTTOM LINE ... SAFETY FIRST!

24. Afterword

S hooting is a lot of fun. It can also be deadly serious. I often sign my books "Safe Shooting." This isn't just a saying, it is a mindset—a reminder to always be safe. I also tell people, "Practice like your life may depend on it." Again, this is not a platitude but a reminder. This is a sport, and this is something we do for fun, but if the worst happens, are you and your skills ready to defend yourself and your family? I truly hope you never have to find out. But isn't it better to be prepared?

If you are looking for more training, consider Personal Defense Readiness (PDR) or Krav Maga to enhance your unarmed defensive skills. Remember, everything you learn unarmed you can use to buy time to get away or get to your gun.

Thank you for taking this journey with me. You can send me comments or questions at FemaleandArmed@Gmail.com or Female and Armed on Facebook. Stay safe, have fun in your training, and always be aware of your surroundings. Remember, your best defense is to avoid a confrontation, so trust your instincts.

Safe Shooting!

Just for fun, here are some of the pictures of us at the range.

Figure 63 - Amy

Figure 64 - Judy

Figure 65 - Kathleen

Figure 66 - Judit

Figure 67 - Lynne

Figure 68 - Ed

Figure 69 - Noah

Figure 70 - Christine

Figure 71 - Don

Figure 72 - Emergency Kit

Figure 73 - Water Jug

About the Author:

Lynne Finch is the author of two other books from Skyhorse Publishing, *Taking Your First Shot* and *The Home Security Handbook*. She is a contributing writer for *Combat Handgun Magazine*, as well as her blog, www.FemaleandArmed.blogspot.com. Lynne holds multiple NRA credentials, as well as a Defensive Firearms Coach certification from ICE Training. She has also developed a seminar on unarmed defensive tactics for women.

Figure 74 - Lynne Finch

Lynne has a day job with the federal government and manages her training company, Female and Armed, a division of F&A, LLC, in the evenings and on weekends. Her business model is home-based training parties—similar to Tupperware but with guns. She believes this offers a more relaxed, smaller class environment; usually the hostess will invite friends, so they know each other. Plus, since we do most of our gun handling, loading, cleaning, and storing in the home, what better place to discuss topics such as safe direction? For her, it is about the passion for sharing knowledge and empowering women to feel safer in a scary world. She has also conducted seminars in small retail shops for employees and been a guest on a Maryland Public Access TV show to talk about writing and self-defense.

She shares her home in Northern Virginia with two loving rescue cats, Rhiannon and Cinnia.

Her website is www.FemaleandArmed.com.